Can you Touch a Rainbow?

Sue Nicholson

Illustrated by Lalalimola

Can I stand on a cloud?

No! Some clouds may look like **thick, fluffy** balls of cotton wool but if you tried to stand on one...

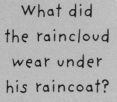

What did the raincloud wear under his raincoat?

Thunderwear!

...you'd **fall** right through it!

Clouds are made up of **millions** of **teeny tiny** drops of water or ice.

If the drops get big and heavy, they fall as rain or snow.

If fluffy white **cumulus** clouds turn grey and grow taller and taller — run! A storm is coming!

Long, grey **stratus** clouds bring the rain, so don't forget your umbrella!

Can you **spot** the **Know-it-all owl** and **owlets** as you read this book?

Can a plant eat a lion?

No, a plant couldn't eat a huge lion but some **greedy plants** eat smaller animals, such as a tasty fly or an ant.

A fly lands on a **Venus Flytrap**, then

SNAP!

The plant's leaves snap shut, trapping the fly inside.

An ant lands on a
pitcher plant's
slippery side...

...then **slides** inside...

...and is turned into
a **soupy mush**.
Yuk!

Fancy that...
It takes a Venus Flytrap
about **10 days**
to digest a
whole fly!

Where do rivers go?

Most rivers start as a **tiny trickle** of water high in the mountains and end up in the salty sea.

Water from rainclouds or melted snow trickles down the mountain in a stream.

START

The stream joins other streams, and collects more and more water until it becomes a **deep, wide river.**

FINISH

Some rivers end up in lakes.

Most rivers end up in the sea or ocean.

Does the wind whistle?

When you're tucked up in bed, have you ever heard the wind whistling or even shrieking like a monster?

Don't worry, the wind isn't alive and can't really whistle. What you can hear is the sound of the air **rushing** from one place to another.

Have you heard the wind whistling through the trees?

Leaves **crackle**, twigs **rustle** and branches creak.

On a stormy day, branches may **SNAP**.

On a really stormy day, trees may **CRASH** to the ground!

Do mountains grow?

Yes, many mountains grow. The world's **highest** mountain, Mount Everest, is growing a few millimetres every year.

Mount Everest is **8,848** metres high. That's about as high as **125** jumbo jets laid end to end!

What do you call a mountain with hiccups?

A volcano!

Mount Everest is growing because it's being pushed up by huge pieces of rock, which **CRASH** and **crumple** into each other underneath it.

Are snowflakes made of ice cream?

Squelch through the squidgy snow in your wellies.
What do you think it's made of?
Maybe it's ice cream...

NO! Snowflakes are made when tiny drops of water in the clouds **freeze** into **ice**. The bits of ice bump into each other and stick together to make snowflakes.

When the snowflakes get **BIG** and **heavy**, they fall to the ground as snow.

Can you spot **six** differences between these two snowflakes?

Every snowflake has **six sides** and each one is **different.**

What did the big, furry hat say to the warm, woolly scarf?

You hang around, whilst I go on ahead!

Why do leaves fall off trees?

Leaves fall off trees because the trees don't need them anymore!

Float!

Soft leaves can get damaged in the cold winter months, so the trees use up all the green food that's left in them, then...

Flutter

...their leaves fall off.

Can you count how many leaves have fallen from the tree? Is it 5, 10 or 12?

Many leaves are blown away in the wind.

Fly!

The trees grow new leaves when it's warmer in the spring.

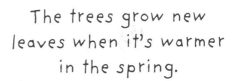

Evergreen trees **never** lose their leaves. They live in warm, wet places or have needles, which don't get damaged when it's cold or dry.

Where do puddles go?

You'll see lots of puddles on a rainy day but be **quick** if you want to jump in one. Puddles soon disappear when the rain stops, especially when the sun comes out!

The **hot** sun warms the water and turns it into a steam called **water vapour**, which **escapes** into the air.

splish!

splash!

splosh

Sometimes the water soaks away into the ground.

Puddles don't appear in a **light, slow drizzle**...

...but in a **fast, heavy** shower, puddles can be huge!

What wakes a volcano?

BANG!

A volcano wakes up when hot, runny rock called **magma** creeps **up** and **up** and **up** through cracks inside, then... BANG!

The magma bursts out and the volcano explodes, or erupts. This is called an **active volcano**.

A **dormant** volcano is sleeping. But don't be fooled. If the magma inside finds a way to the surface, the volcano may wake up with a

CRASH!

A volcano is **extinct** when it has no magma left inside. This means it won't ever erupt again.

Does the Earth have a roof?

The Earth doesn't have a roof because the sky doesn't end.
The gases that make up the sky get thinner and thinner,
and s p r e a d   o u t until **space** begins.

The Earth looks like a beautiful green-blue ball from space.

The sky is another name for the **atmosphere** – it's a blanket of gases around the Earth.

A strong force called **gravity** stops the atmosphere — and you — floating off into space!

Gravity pulls you down to the ground when you jump up in the air.

Will I need my umbrella in the desert?

No, you **won't** need to pack your umbrella, because deserts are **dry** places where it hardly ever rains. But a big sunshade would protect you from the burning sun, if you could fit one in your suitcase!

What is a camel's favourite nursery rhyme?

Humpty Dumpty!

Even though deserts can be sizzling hot in the day, they can get **icy cold** at night. Sometimes, it even **snows!** Brrrr!

The driest desert in the world is the **Dry Valleys** in Antarctica. It hasn't rained there for **TWO million years**. Now that's a loooooong time!

Can I drink seawater?

No, don't **ever** try to drink seawater
— unless you're a fish, of course.

The sea is full of salt
— and too much salt
can make you ill.

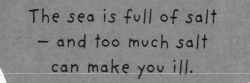

Why did the
fish blush?

Because the
sea weed!

There's about a
tablespoonful of salt
in one glass of seawater.

The sea is salty because tiny salty pieces of rock called **minerals** are washed from the land into the sea.

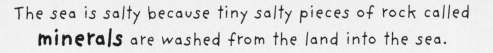

Earth has five **oceans** – the Pacific, Atlantic, Indian, Southern and Arctic Oceans.

Land ahoy!

The **sea** is the name given to the parts of the oceans nearest to land.

Does it rain a lot in the rainforest?

Yes, every day's a rainy day in a tropical rainforest. Tropical rainforests are **warm** and **steamy**, too.

Towering trees can grow up to 60 metres tall — that's as high as 12 houses stacked on top of each other.

In the **thick leafy** part of the rainforest the trees' leaves join up in a canopy, like a **GIANT green umbrella**. Can you spot a sleepy sloth and a scuttling spider?

It can take raindrops around 10 minutes to **pitter patter** through the trees down to the forest floor.

plants have babies?

Plants don't have babies, but they do have **seeds**, which grow into baby plants called **seedlings.**

Plants don't look after their babies the way we do but they do make sure their seeds have plenty of food to help them grow.

There are lots of ways seeds travel to find a new place to **grow**.

Some roll along the ground.

Some hitch a ride on an animal's fur!

Some float on the ocean waves.

Some fly on feathery parachutes or tiny wings!

Can I touch a rainbow?

No, because rainbows are made of light, and you can't touch light.

A rainbow appears when sunlight shines through drops of water, which splits the light into different colours.

Which two paint colours for the rainbow are missing?

orange

yellow

green

violet

indigo

What lives at the bottom of the sea?

MILLIONS of creatures live just under the waves, from fabulous **fish** and dancing **dolphins**, to slippery **sharks** and spiky **starfish**...

...but as the land drops **down**, **down**, **down**, **down**

to the seabed (sea floor)...

...past smoking
volcanoes...

...and into deep, dark **trenches**,
where it's pitch black and icy cold,
no one is quite sure what weird and
wonderful creatures live here!

The Sun is a
GIGANTIC
ball of swirling, super-hot
exploding gases. One of the
gases is called **hydrogen**.
As the hydrogen gas explodes,
it blasts heat and light
into space.

Never look at the
Sun, as it will
damage your eyes.

Without the Sun's heat and light, the Earth would be cold and dark, with no plants or animals.

Why did the Sun go to school?

To get brighter!

Fancy that...
If the Earth were any closer to the Sun, it would burn to a crisp!

Why does lightning zigzag?

Lightning is a huge *flash* of electricity that leaps from a cloud in a thunderstorm. It zigzags as it finds the shortest, and quickest way through the air to the ground.

Try this...

Take a bucket of water outside and find some sloping ground covered in stones and dirt. Pour some water on the slope. What do you see?

What happens...

The water zigzags down the slope as it runs around stones and dirt. Just like lightning, the water finds the easiest way down.

Why is the sky blue?

Sunlight looks white but it's actually made up of all seven colours of the rainbow!

The blue light is **scattered** across the sky more than the other colours...

...which is why the sky looks blue.

Never look at the Sun, as it will damage your eyes.

As the blue light gets further from the sun it is scattered more and more. So by the time it reaches us it's spread very thinly and the sky looks pale blue or even white.

In the evening, at **sunset** when the Sun is low in the sky, the red and orange colours are scattered more.

Is anywhere colder than my freezer?

Yes, Antarctica is the **coldest** place on the Earth. In winter, the temperature is a freezing **−60°C** Brrr! That's **three times colder** than your freezer!

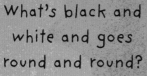

What's black and white and goes round and round?

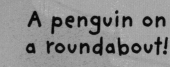

A penguin on a roundabout!

Most of Antarctica is
covered in **thick ice** over
1.6 kilometres deep. That's
as deep as 50 blue whales
laid nose to tail!

Fancy that...
Penguins sneeze to get rid of
a lot of the salty seawater they
swallow with their fishy meals.

Why does thunder make me jump?

Thunder is the noise made by lightning in a thunderstorm. It can be a long, deep **rumbling** and **grumbling** in the distance, or a huge **CRACK** that makes you jump it's **so loud!**

RUM

RUMBLE!

Lightning makes a noise because it heats up the air around it, which then **explodes** in a **huge**

CRASH!

RUMBLE!

You see lightning before you hear thunder because light travels *faster* than sound through the air.

Can plants dance?

Plants may look like they're dancing when they **swish** and **sway** in the wind, but they can't breakdance or do ballet!

These **swishing, swaying** sunflowers turn their faces to the Sun as it moves across the sky.

This telegraph plant is sometimes called a **dancing plant** because its leaves dance up and down in the sunshine.

The leaves on this mimosa plant fold in when you touch them, as if they are **taking a bow**.

Where do stars go in the morning?

Nowhere – they are still there, high in the sky. We just can't see them in the day because the Sun is so **bright**.

The Sun is a star, too. It is the closest star to the Earth.

Even though the Sun is our closest star, it is still a long way away. If you drove there non-stop, it would take you **over 100 years!**

Never look at the Sun, as it will damage your eyes.

The stars you can see at night are **hot, glowing** balls of **gas,** like our Sun.

Super-hot stars look white or blue.

Stars can live for **billions** of years.

Older, colder stars may look orange or red.

What kind of stars wear sunglasses?

Film stars!

THINGS to MAKE and DO

Watch the weather Draw a simple chart with squares, one for each day of the month. Add little pictures to show how the weather changes day by day. For example, draw a snowflake or the Sun coming out from behind a cloud.

Make snowflakes

Fold squares of paper as shown below, then snip away sections to make six-pointed snowflakes. Fix the snowflakes to a window or glue onto coloured card.

Make a leafy tree collage

Paint the trunk and bare branches of a tree on thick paper or card. When the paint is dry, glue on bits of scrunched-up tissue paper to make leaves. Do you want to make it green for summer or red, yellow and brown for autumn?

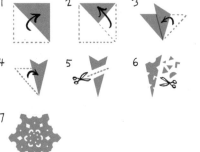

Go star-gazing Wrap up warm and go outside with your grown-up on a clear, moonless night to look at the stars. See if you can spot a shooting star!

Quarto is the authority on a wide range of topics.

Quarto educates, entertains and enriches the lives of our readers—enthusiasts and lovers of hands-on living.

www.quartoknows.com

MIX
Paper from responsible sources
FSC® C104723

A catalogue record for this book is available from the British Library.

ISBN 978 1 78493 836 9

Author: Sue Nicholson
Illustrations © Sandra Navarro/Lalalimola 2017
Editors: Carly Madden and Catherine Veitch
Designer: Victoria Kimonidou

Printed in China
10 9 8 7 6 5 4 3 2 1